A GLIMPSE
OF THE FREED MIND

KARL-HEINZ SCHRADT

AUTHOR / ARTWORK
Karl-Heinz Schradt

© 2018 Galah Books
© 2018 Karl-Heinz Schradt

All rights reserved. No part of this publication may be reproduced, distributed, or transmitted in any form or by any means, including photocopying, recording, or other electronic or mechanical methods, without the prior written permission of the publisher, except in the case of brief quotations embodied in critical reviews and specific other non-commercial uses permitted by copyright law. For permission requests, write to the publisher:
Email:galahbooks@hotmail.com
Facebook: www.facebook.com/Galahbookspublisher

www.galahbooks.com
Ordering Information available on our website.

A GLIMPSE
OF THE FREED MIND

KARL-HEINZ SCHRADT

INTRODUCTION

There are multiple paths to enlightenment. This book does not claim to be one such path but does aim to provide a glimpse of what Awakening may look like from one of many perspectives. The underlying assumption is that multiple viewpoints are valid and asserts no unusual or magical understanding of the issue.

The ideas contained in this book are drawn from, or inspired by, many of the traditional philosophies from the East, such as Buddhism, Hinduism and Wu Wei. To ensure balance, many Western writers and philosophers who were inspired by these great Eastern traditions have also influenced this book. Beyond its origins, this book offers a unifying vision: a way in which many of the world's spiritual, philosophical and religious ideas can exist in complete harmony. It focuses on what is familiar and shared, regarding what we know, while minimising the specifics and details that too often separate and fracture communities and opinions. It is a story of personal and universal healing and reconnection.

Awakening or enlightenment can be defined in many ways, and the goal of this book is to contribute to the discussion. One assumption when pursuing a path to Awakening is that Awakening is an end that is achieved and done with. Here, Awakening is seen as an ongoing process in which a person does not solve and overcome their life's problems but instead changes the way we approach and understand them. It invites new ways of being to end destructive and damaging cycles of behaviour that make suffering worse. Further, it encourages the formation or adoption, and gradual mastery of techniques of being that serve a positive relationship with the world rather than alienation from it. Whatever your background and personal challenges, I hope this book offers you enjoyment and a chance for reflection.

Yours,

Karl-Heinz Schradt

You exist.

Earth, exists; as do trees, animals and other people...

...also stars, planets and galaxies in their various types exist...

Consider all of these things and anything else you know of, or could imagine or suppose....

...you would have something that you could call 'Everything'

'Everything' could also be called:

You can decide which term suits you best.

It will hence be referred to as:

Which stands for '[The] Infinite' Or 'Infinity'.

As stated, because ∞ is everything, everything can be found in, or comes from ∞.

Each thing is part of the greater ∞ and cannot be cut away from the rest of ∞...

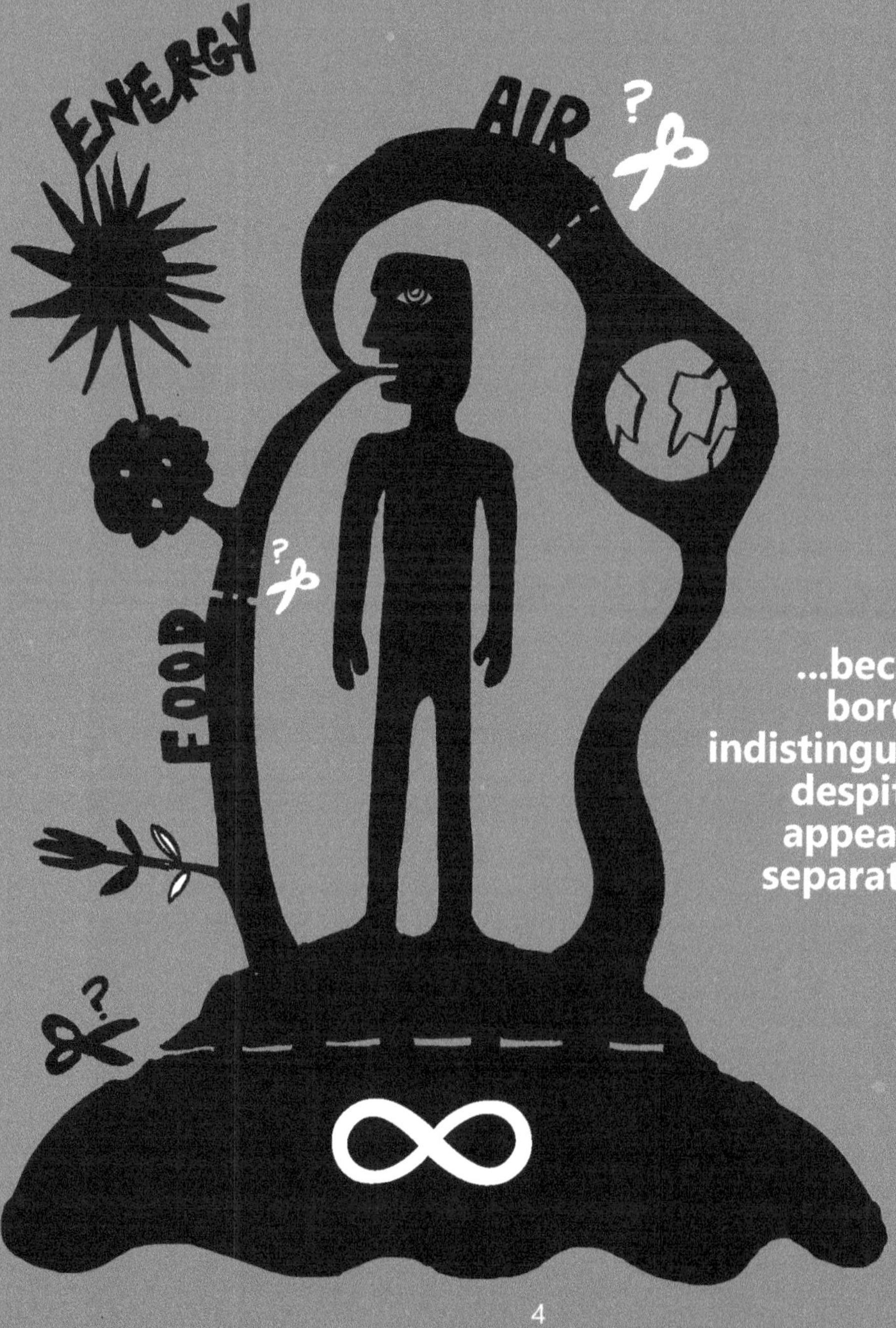

...because the borders are indistinguishable, despite often appearing like separate things.

Despite this connection, we can only experience ourselves.

Like a head on a coin, we need to explore or turn the coin...

...there is another side which is everything else and every-one else...

...both sides make the whole...

...because of this situation, we sometimes fall into thinking that we are alone in a cold, unfriendly world that we 'came into' when we were born...

...but we are not alone... we were never separated...

...so if you ever feel lonely, remember - you came from this world... and are not a stranger in it...

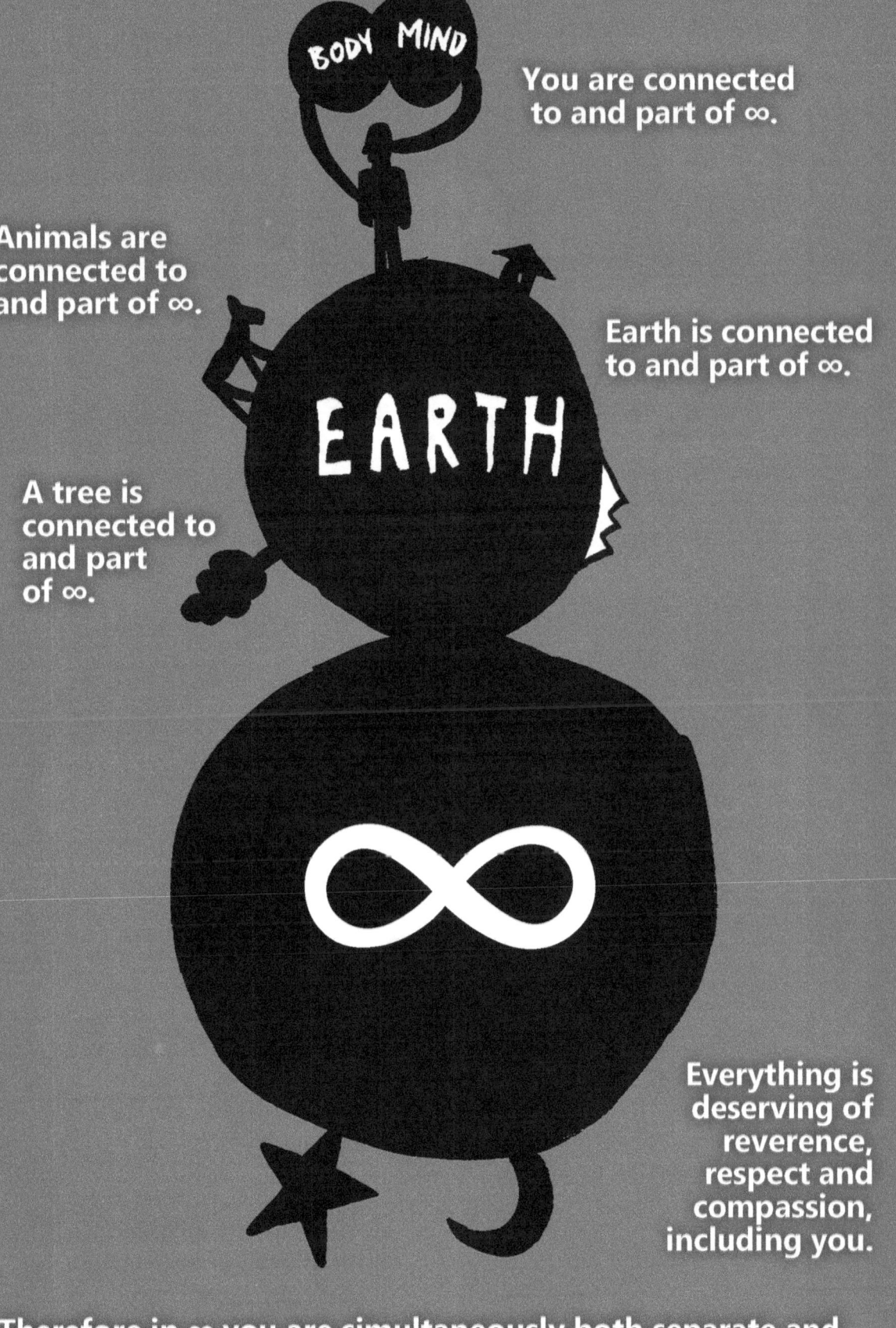

We see that we have intelligence as sentient beings, as do other living things...

Both animals and humans can think, feel and respond, and are therefore sentient.

A human or animal therefore, is ∞ being aware of itself.

When we admire remarkable beauty, we are experiencing the awesome feeling...

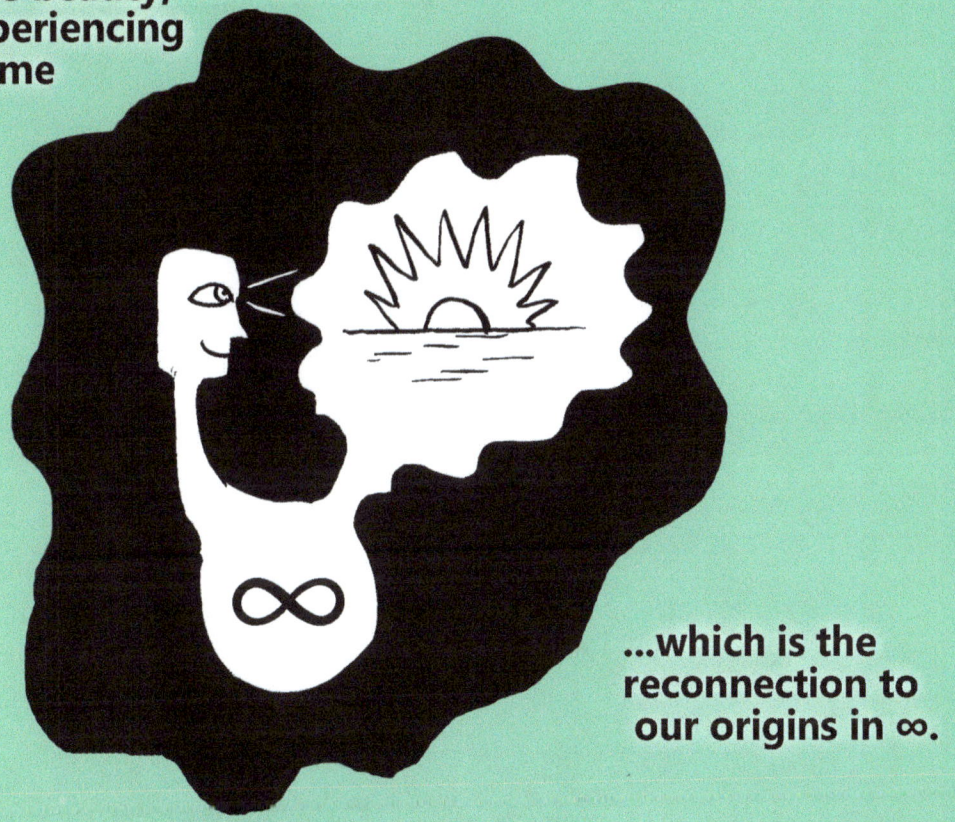

...which is the reconnection to our origins in ∞.

You are ∞, knowing itself.

You can see the ∞ in you...

...when you are open to seeing it.

Others are ∞ and you can see ∞ in them, when you are ready to see it.

We see the ∞ is others. We all are ∞.

This is the ∞.

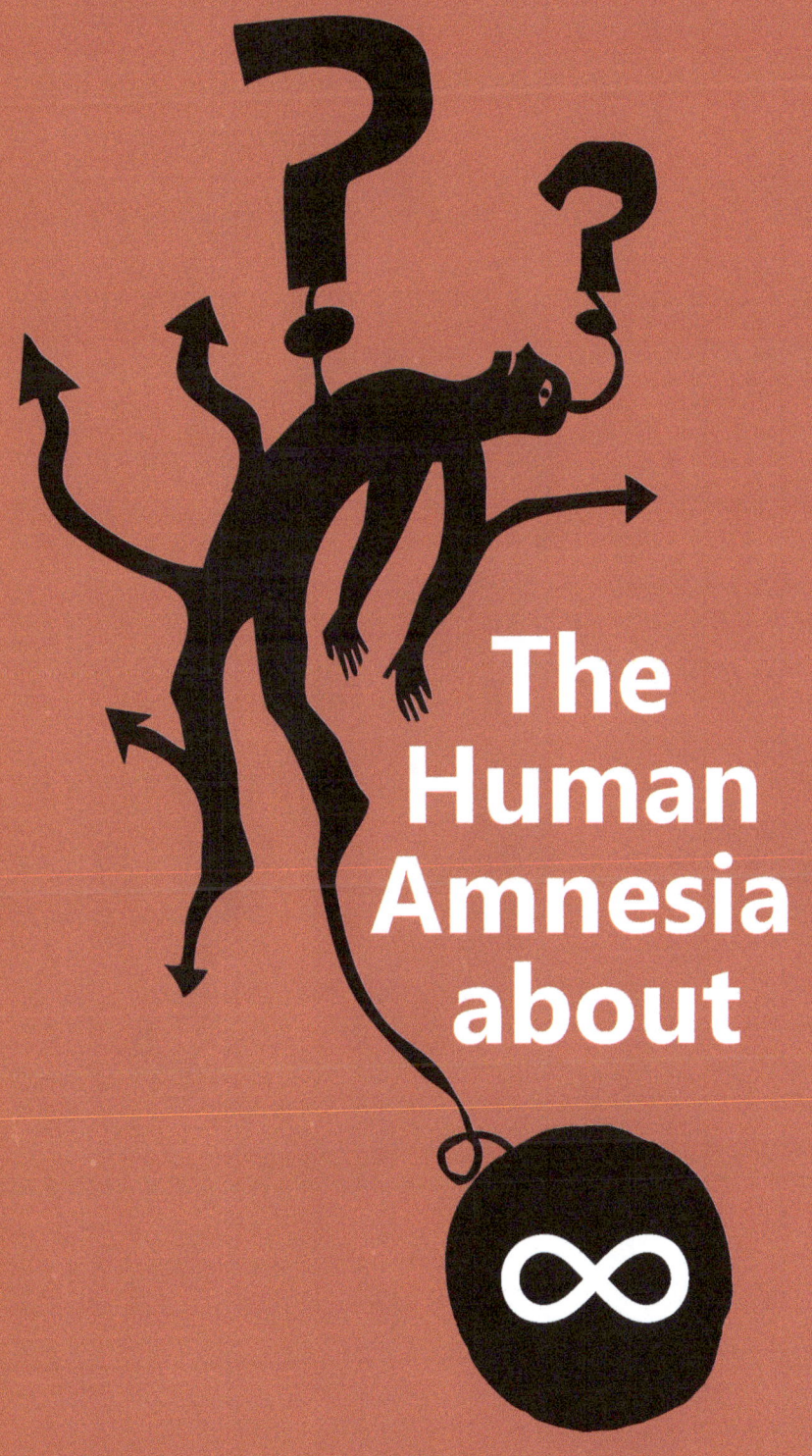

The Human Amnesia about ∞

We are told by others who arrived in the ages before us why we are here and what we must do...

We use the information we are given to make ourselves into a person...

The word 'person' comes from the Greek persona, which means mask. It is this mask we present to the world as 'self'...

...there are masks we use to fit in...

...though some choose a mask to 'fit out' instead...

...either way both are masks...

The mask is helpful because it assists us with getting on with others we agree with...

...or makes us feel justified in being alone.

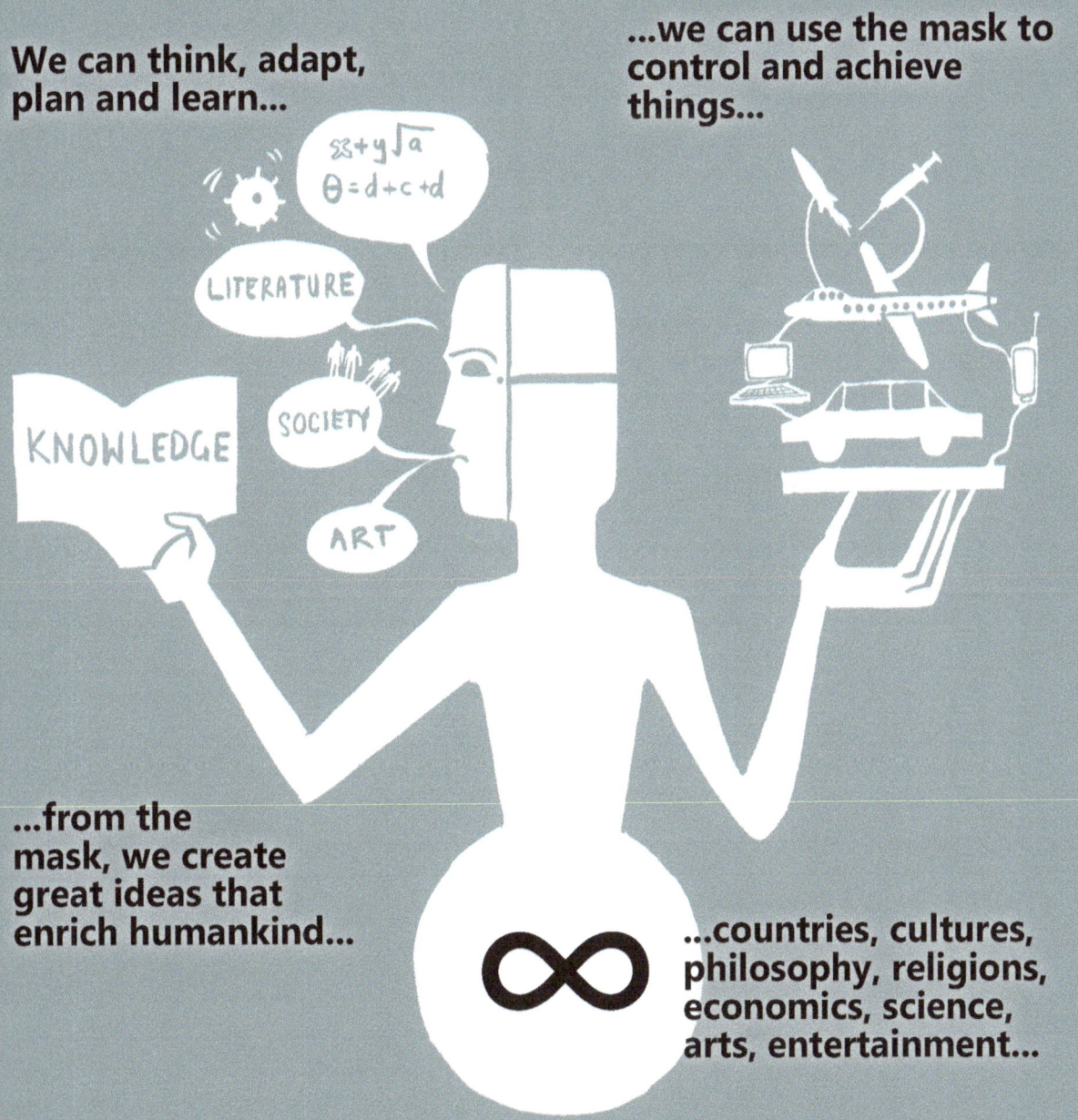

$$x+y\sqrt{a}$$
$$\theta = d+c+d$$

LITERATURE

KNOWLEDGE

SOCIETY

ART

MATHS

The Choking Mask

The collective wearing of the mask becomes a serious business we call 'society'...

...in which we are obsessed by how others perceive us and keep our masks as we think they would want them...

...the various masks include 'a real success' 'a real man', 'a real woman' and rebellious masks like 'renegade'...

...but none of these masks are actually what we are...

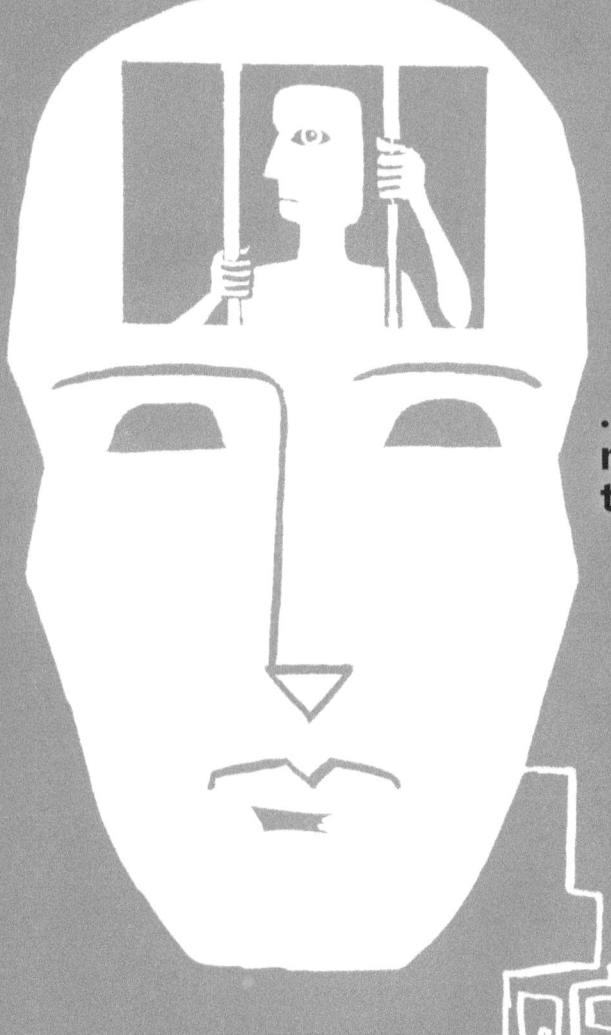

If we get too connected to our persona, we begin to forget...

...that the mask is not 'truth' or reality in and of itself...

...we forget that we may have freedom to shape the mask...

...or we forget more and more that we are connected to the ∞, and to Earth, nature and other people...

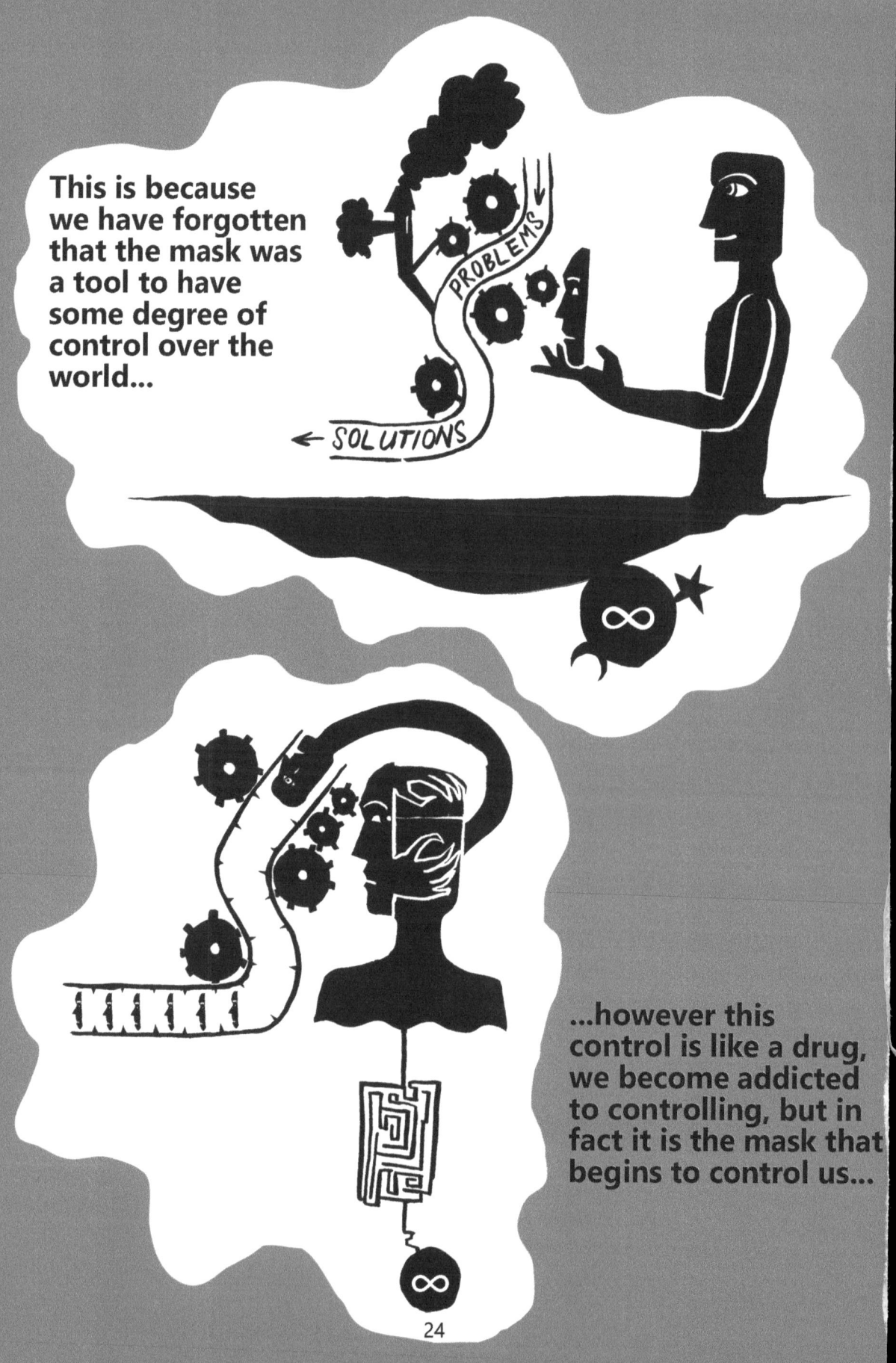

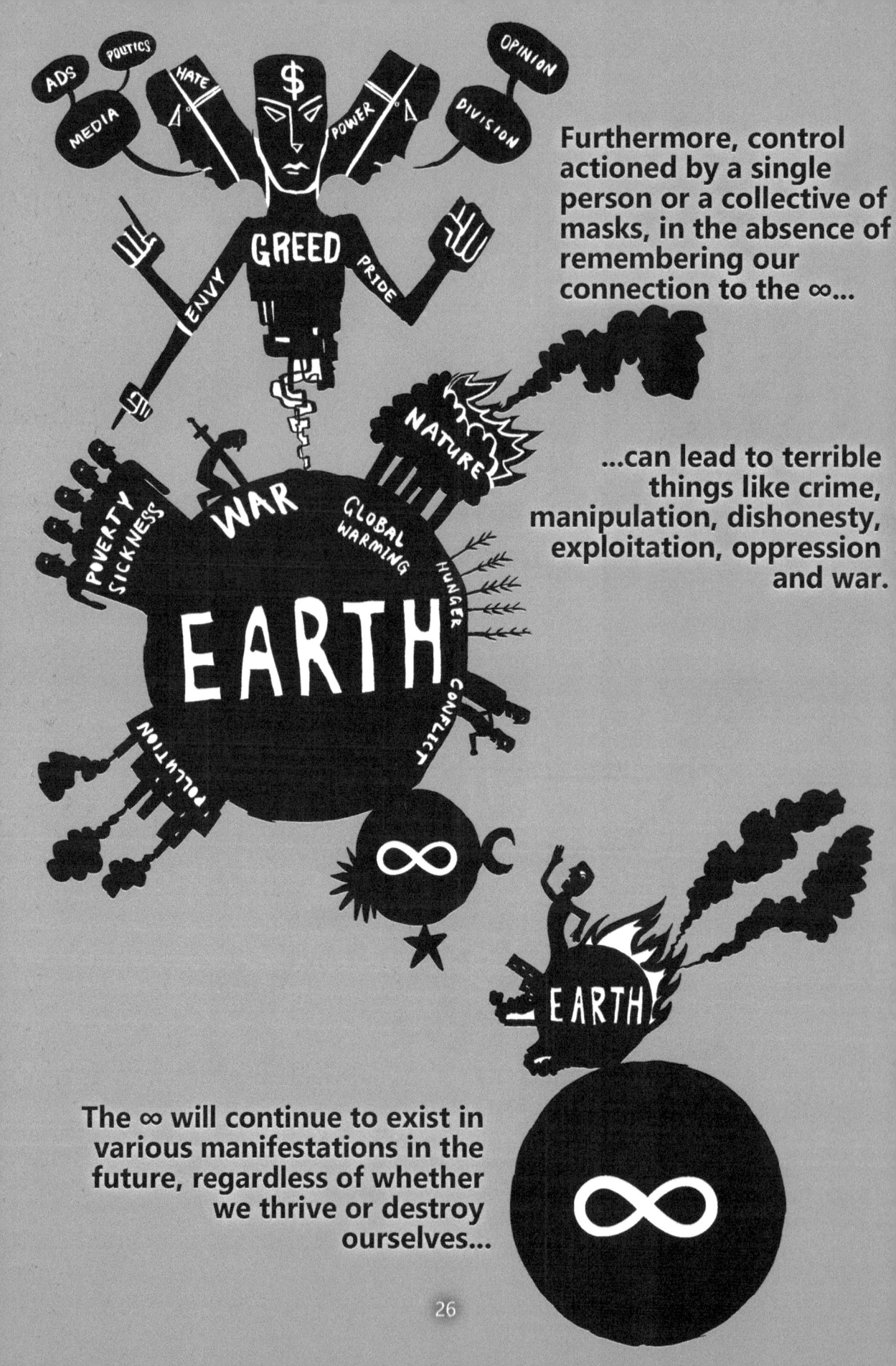

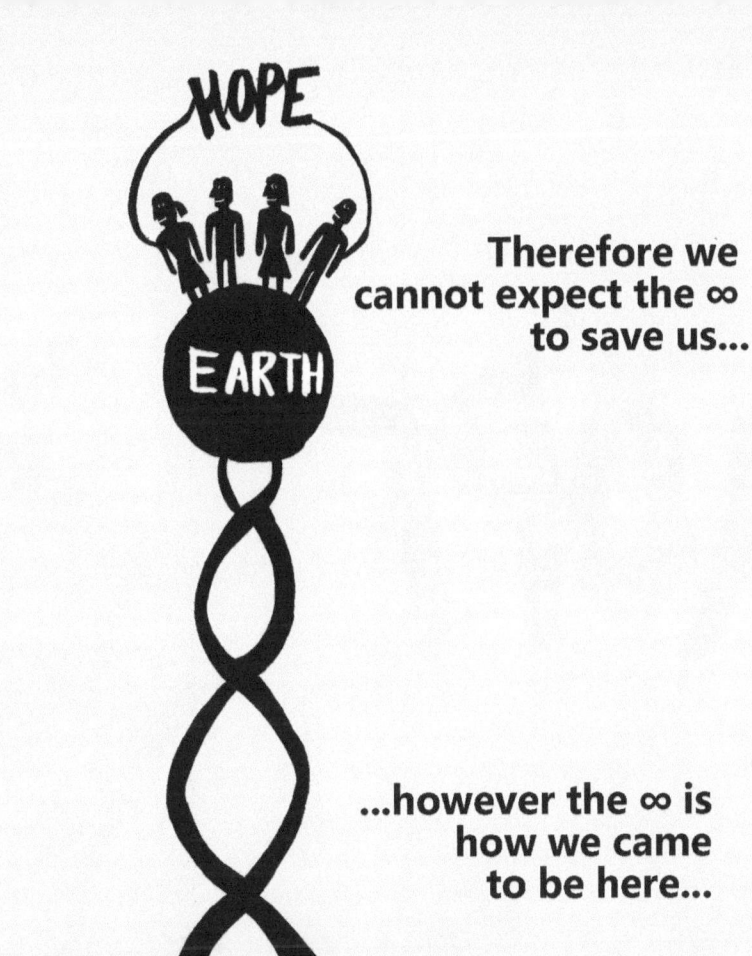

Therefore we cannot expect the ∞ to save us...

...however the ∞ is how we came to be here...

...it has given us the tools to save ourselves.

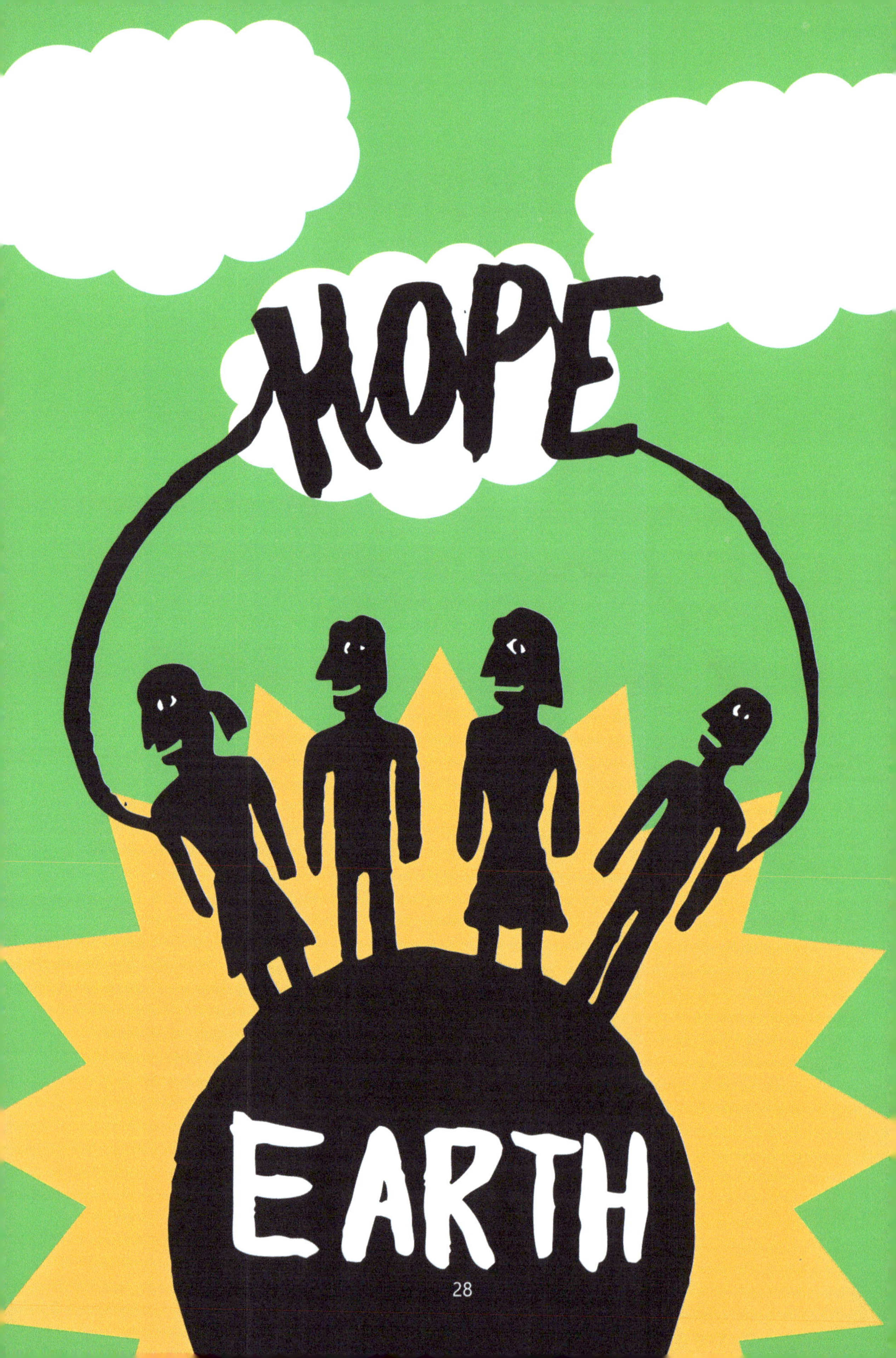
HOPE
EARTH

The Challenge

The Mask or Persona is also sometimes known as the 'Ego-Self' or our 'Identity'.

The Ego-self tends to be fixed to titles like a name, an occupation, a perceived status and a set of fixed and inflexible beliefs...

...whereas the ∞ self, like the Infinite, is not fixed at all...

The ∞ self is changing moment by moment...

...thoughts and feelings come and go, and are always changing...

Because of this state of change, nothing is rigidly attached to or identified with.

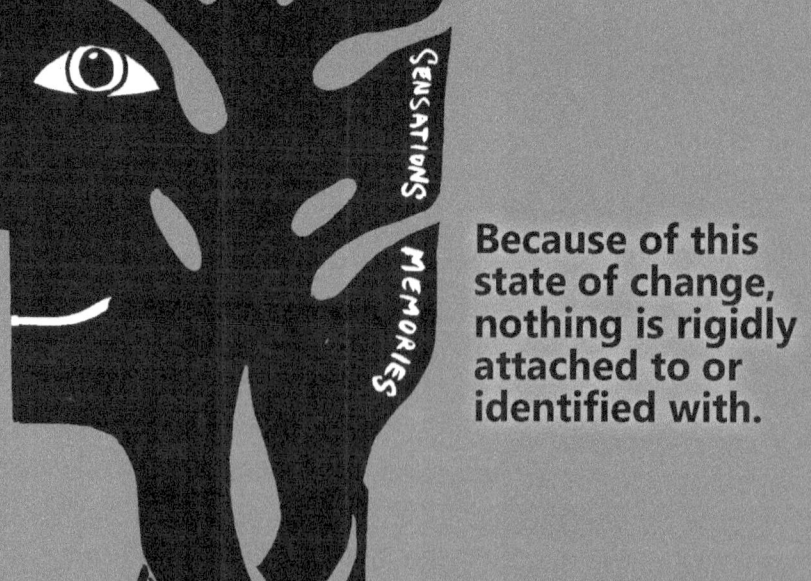

For this reason the ∞ self is peaceful, tranquil, unruffled and spontaneous...

...we actually must be both the ∞ self and the human mask at the same time.

To be too attached to the Persona, its thoughts and its feelings is to become stale and inflexible to the changing of the ∞...

Whilst everything appears to be great on the outside...

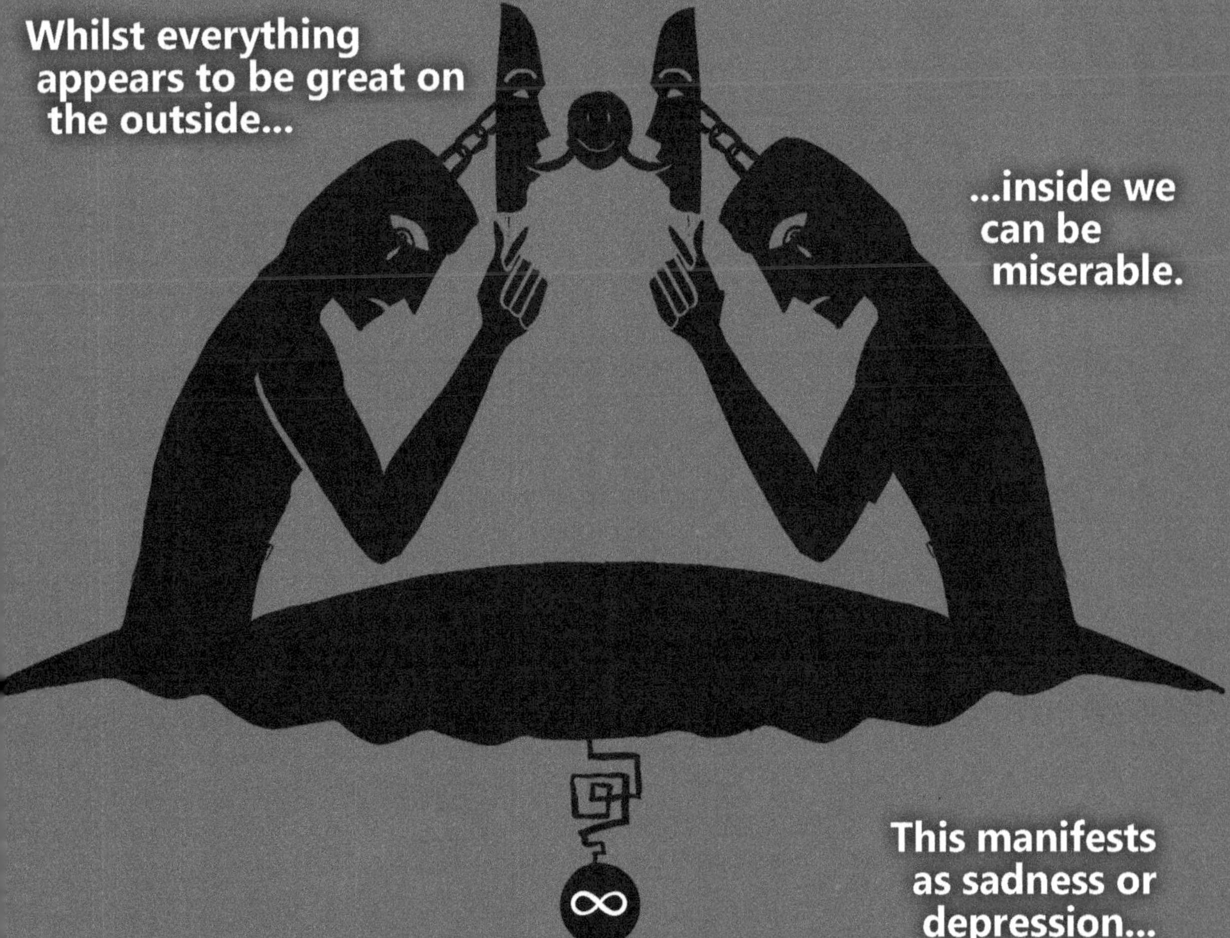

...inside we can be miserable.

This manifests as sadness or depression...

Anxiety has been described as the feeling that results when we either have a conflict between the mask and the ∞ self...

...or we are flipping quickly between the two, unsure of what we are feeling.

...We can start by noticing and experiencing this inner conflict, without judging it as either right or wrong.

Abandoning the mask entirely is not an answer as we need it to exist as a human.

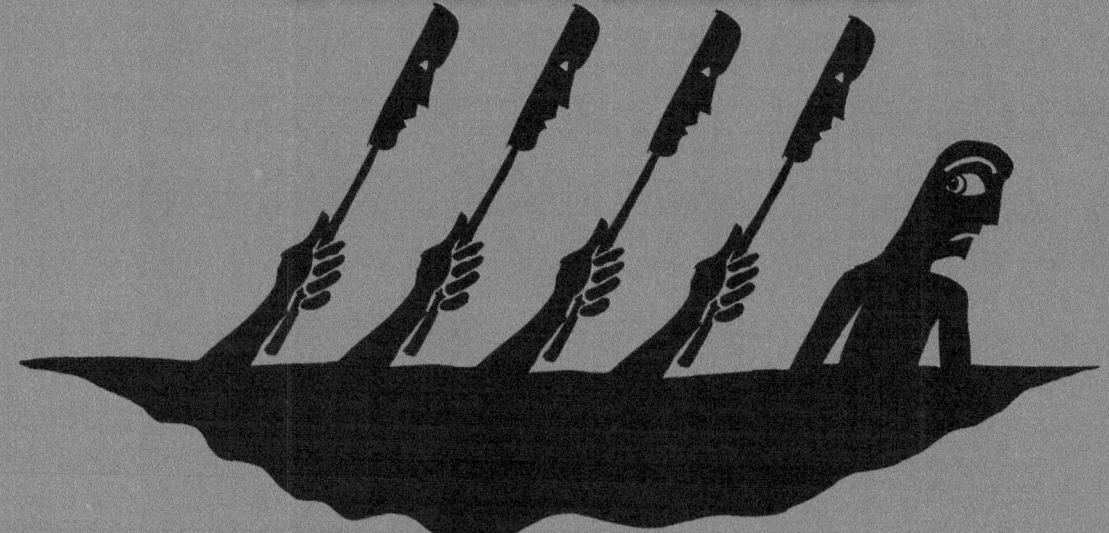

One of the uses of the mask is that it is a shell that helps us feel less vulnerable in an often frightening world...

To be only the ∞ alone would be to not be a functioning human at all...

Some try to become nothing and attempt to cease to exist, but this is a trap too...

An Awakened person understands both 'good products' and 'good processes' have value...

...and that a good process, being fair and compassionate...

...also tends to have a good outcome...

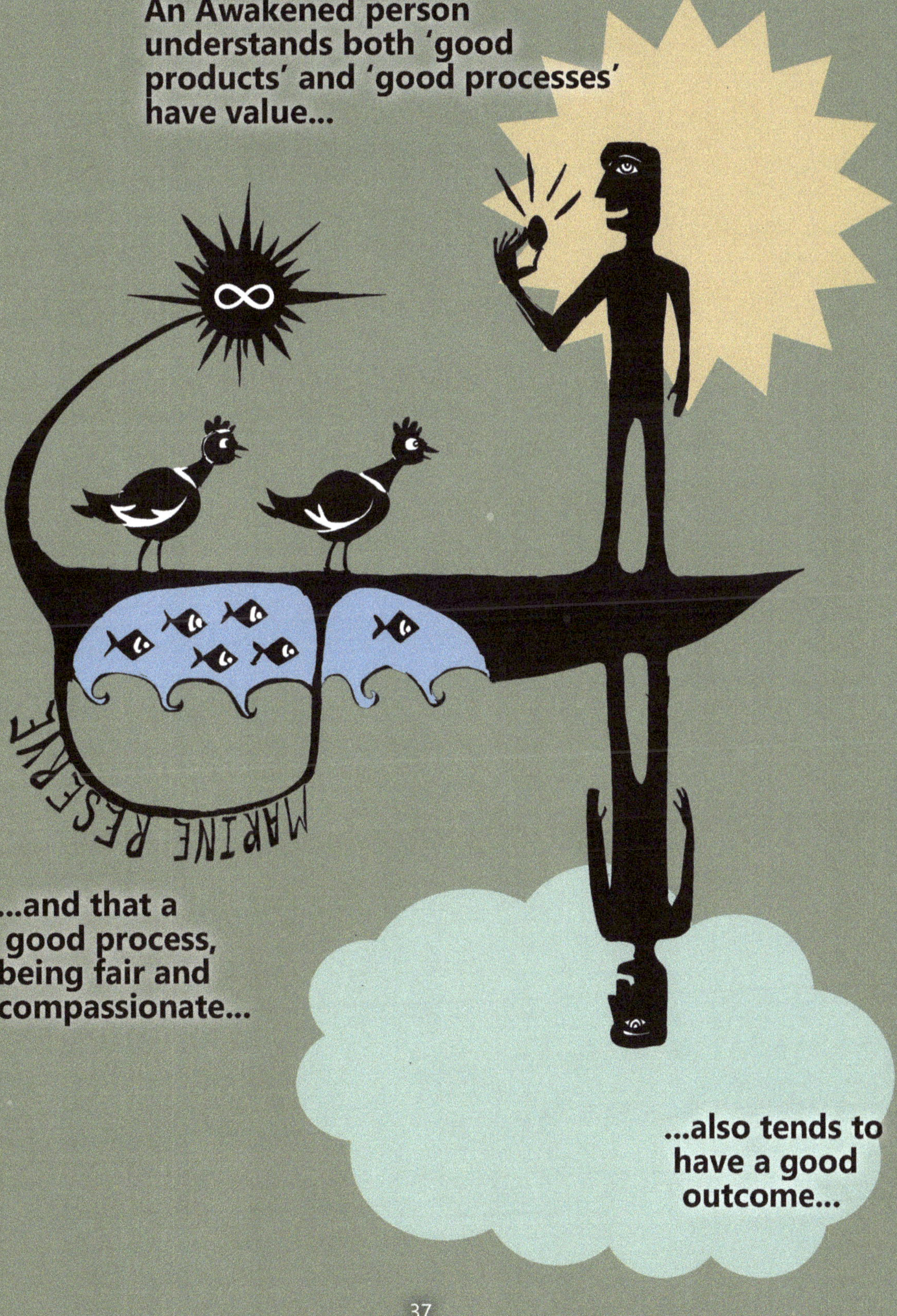

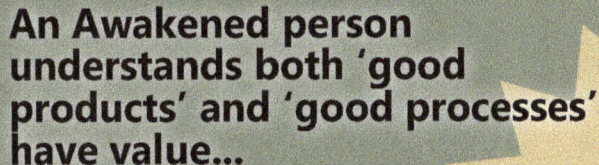

Returning

...it only needs to be freed.

Reconnecting to ∞ reminds us that we need not believe all the mask's thoughts...

...and we can discover our underlying nature....

...and also understand that the mask is necessary and normal. We start learning to be kind to it and ourselves...

..Reconnecting also helps us recognise our mask from the ∞ self...

...Although this can take some time...

Reconnecting can happen in so many ways...

The first part is being open to reconnecting, having the right attitude...

...almost any experience can connect us if we have the willingness to see the ∞ in what we are doing...

...we begin to see the amazing in everything, whether talking, playing music, doing maths and so on.

Sometimes the mask makes 'feeling content' into an object to be chased....

...or thinks of contentment as a secret that must be discovered...

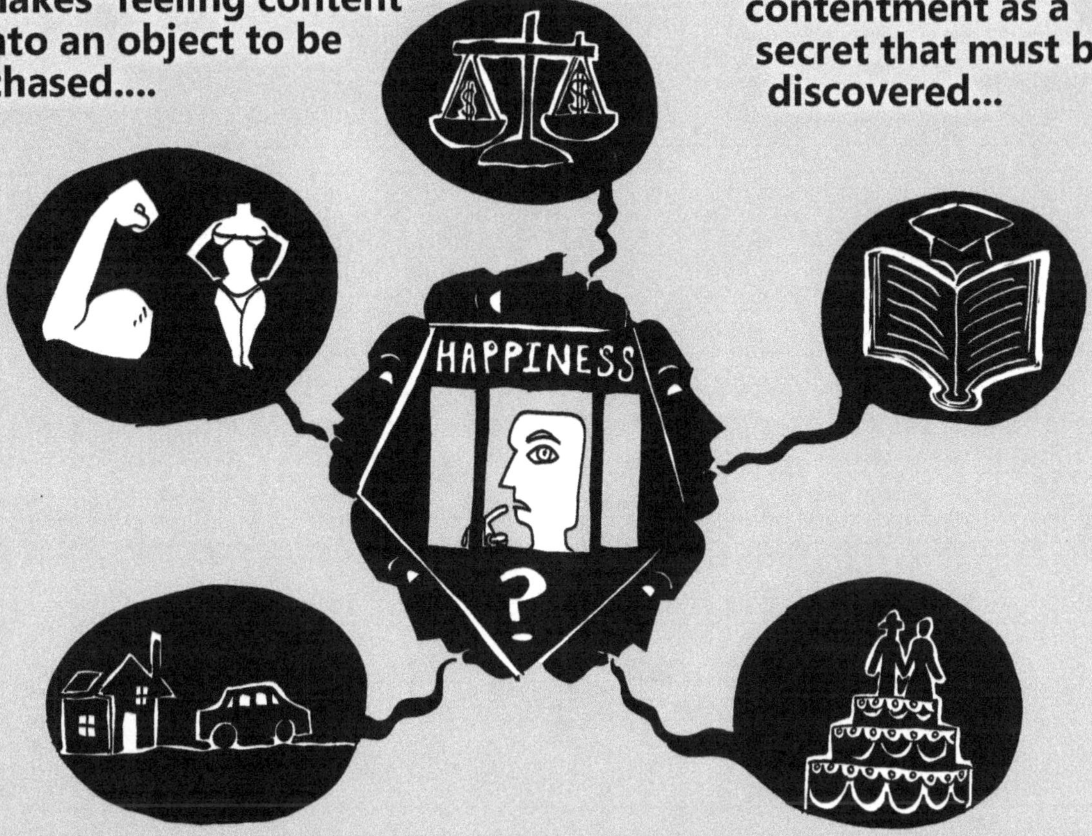

...However contentment is neither -

...To be a content person...

...is like being a good apple...

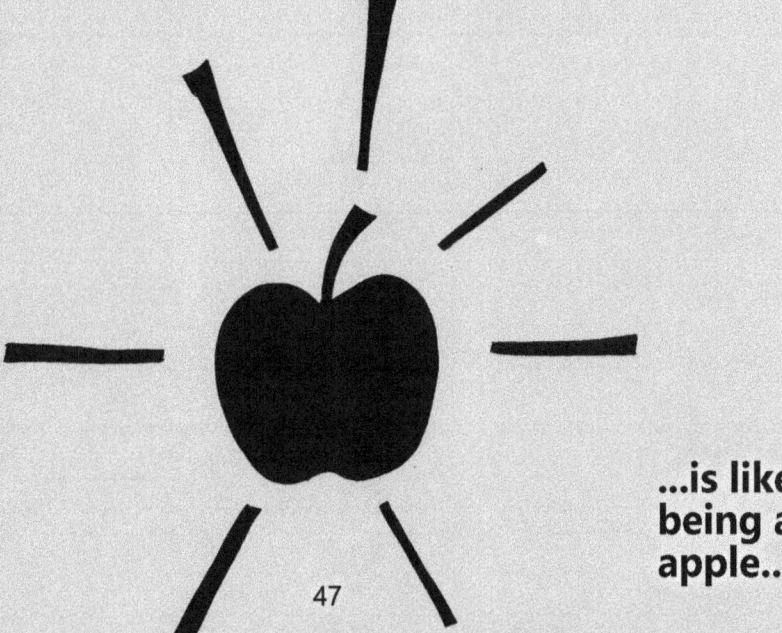

An apple does not need to try to be an apple...

...neither does it need to put effort into being a 'good apple'...

Similarly, the effort of the mask doesn't make a person good.

When we reconnect to our naturally Awakened selves and let go of the Persona...

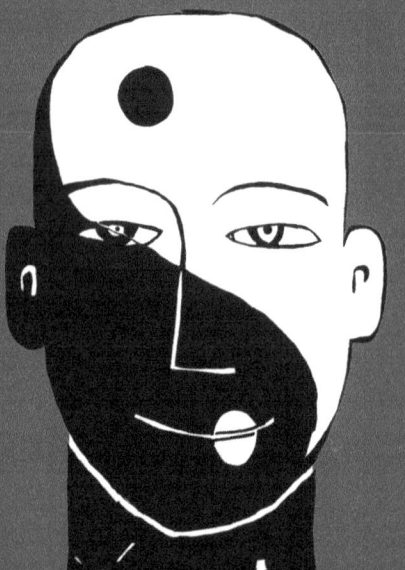

...and cease trying..

...goodness just happens.

We make time for the task, and are disciplined...

...we stop doing what doesn't help us...

...and make time for a connection to happen naturally...

...we manage the process by experiencing the mind with kindness, with patience;

and without excessive striving...

...we can let it be light and enjoyable.

...when we successfully reconnect to the ∞...

...we feel a sense of relief and joy to be free from the rigid mask...

...and we remember that we have a choice about our relationship to it.

The Awakened self is automatically compassionate, wise, patient and grateful...

When we successfully reconnect to the ∞...

...we can understand others more deeply because we know they must wear a mask too...

...we start to feel that maybe everything will be okay...

...we feel compassion for them, because we know that wearing a mask is not always easy...

...we are careful about how we act, speak and have understanding attitudes towards them...

...we see that we are not all that different...

...we are all part of the ∞, part of the same team...

...we share the same core needs, and our differences seem trivial...

We learn to be able to drop the mask and be real...

...even if just for a while.

When we see how ∞, the planet and everything provides for us, how other people work hard to provide us with water, food and services, we become grateful...

...we feel kindness and compassion coming from ∞...

....we are helped and we help...

Returning to the Everyday

When we don the mask again, we remember the mask is not the actual 'us'. The true us is a more magnificent thing...

We return refreshed, more resilient...

...we can live without excessive attachment to how things go, we still exist outside the game of Personas and Masks...

Accepting and Moving Through the World of the Mask:

We are kind to ourselves when we feel trapped by the habits and thoughts of the Persona...

...but we work patiently to let go of them, to become untrapped...

Once we see the trap and the trapped are the same entity - at that moment we are released.

We can act with kindness to others wearing masks, for they act and think out of habit, and not necessarily to spite us...

...We forgive...

...When people are busy with the mask, we gently let them continue, as wearing a mask is a dangerous task, like walking a tight rope...

...many people suffer from a broken mask they are attached to.

The Dance of Change

The magic of reconnecting to the ∞ is...

...that we learn to move with the flow of the ∞, rather than fighting against it...

...We know we are part of a changing ∞ and we are changing too...

...we accept that life is change...

...we learn to dance the dance of change...

...to deal well with other people is to dance the dance well...

...we learn to be compassionate...

...kind and patient. We are more flexible...

...To dance is to not live in the past, nor is it to live in the future...

To dance and be harmonious is to always be falling into the present...

To not dance is to be against the flow...

...this leads to being tossed and turned; and manifests as dissatisfaction and discontentment...

...not being sure if one will dance, or attempting to control the dance with the mask, still leads us to conflict...

...To be awakened is to flow with the dance of the ∞...

...and the transitions of the dance of ∞...

...birth and death are transitions of the dance, the dance we are tied to...

...we come from the dance and return to the ∞...

...and new things come from the dance and return to the ∞ ...all the time - over and over...

...it cannot be outwitted...

THIS GREAT LIFE

FROM ∞

BACK INTO ∞

...only surrendered to...

To Awaken is to Gain Wisdom...

...It is to understand how we have been trapped in the past...

...to learn from our previous pain and suffering...

...to decide not to let the mask have total control - knowing it may tempt us into doing or thinking things we know won't benefit us...

With this simple story of the Infinite, You have glimpsed the Awakened – The Freed Mind.